FLORIDA OASIS

a photographic tour of

HARRY P. LEU GARDENS

FOREWORD BY KATY MOSS WARNER

COOL SPRINGS PRESS
Growing Successful Gardeners™

BRENTWOOD, TENNESSEE

Published by Cool Springs Press
P.O. Box 2828
Brentwood, Tennessee 37024

EAN: 978-1-59186-482-0

Library of Congress Cataloging-in-Publication Data

Florida oasis : a photographic tour of Harry P. Leu Gardens / foreword by Katy Moss Warner.

p. cm.

ISBN 978-1-59186-482-0 (hardcover)

1. Harry P. Leu Gardens (Orlando, Fla.) 2. Harry P. Leu Gardens (Orlando, Fla.)--Pictorial works. 3. Botanical gardens--Florida--Orlando. I. Warner, Katy Moss.

QK73.U62H374 2010

712'.50975924--dc22

2010037566

First Printing 2010
Printed in the United States of America
10 9 8 7 6 5 4 3 2 1

Editor: Cindy Kershner
Art Director: Marc Pewitt

Cover photo by Harry P. Leu Gardens staff: *Camellia japonica* 'Betty Sheffield Supreme'.

Photographs and artwork provided by artists are identified by their name. Contributors include Gene Amoroso, Mary Balanda, Greta Baxter, Ron Caimano, Charles Clark, Jon Conrad, Karen Constantine, Suzanne Darby, Pam Daum, Gina Ferreira, Amy Green, Mason Katzen, Karen Kershaw, Deborah Knispel, Richard Koch, Ellen Linder, Tiffany Martin, Lisa O'Brien, Grayson Olachew, Lea Patenaude, Elaine Pawlikowski, Robert Ravas, Marlene Rimensberger, Joan Sandler, Julia Sigmore, Cindy Sturla, Darlene Torres, Ken Wallace, Kim Warden, Paul Wean, Jilene Williams, Dave Wood, and Ellen Zaslaw. Images not identified with a specific artist were made available by Harry P. Leu Gardens.

ACKNOWLEDGEMENTS

It is with great pleasure that we present *Florida Oasis: A Photographic Tour of Harry P. Leu Gardens*. We decided in the early discussions to make this monograph one that represents the true spirit of Leu Gardens. For that reason we invited many individuals who value the Gardens to send their photographic images and representational art to be considered for inclusion in the book. A jury of members of the Board of Trustees and Gardens' staff viewed every image and scrutinized every application.

Since Leu Gardens belongs to the community, this is the community's book. Made possible by funds donated to the Friends of Harry P. Leu Gardens, Inc. and approved by the Trustees, it was written by regional experts and the artwork is by regional artists. We want to gratefully acknowledge the efforts and hard work of all the artists who took the time to send in their images and who cared enough about Leu Gardens to send us their views of the Gardens from an artist's perspective. I hope you will agree that the following renderings and images offer a small glimpse of what Leu Gardens has to see and do every day.

Mr. and Mrs. Leu were truly visionaries some fifty years ago when they decided to present their home and lovely gardens to Central Florida. So, in honor of the Gardens' golden anniversary, and on behalf of Mayor Dyer, the Orlando City Council, the Harry P. Leu Gardens Board of Trustees, the Gardens' staff, and the artists and writers, please enjoy the very best of Leu Gardens in the pages that follow.

ROBERT BOWDEN
Executive Director

CONTENTS

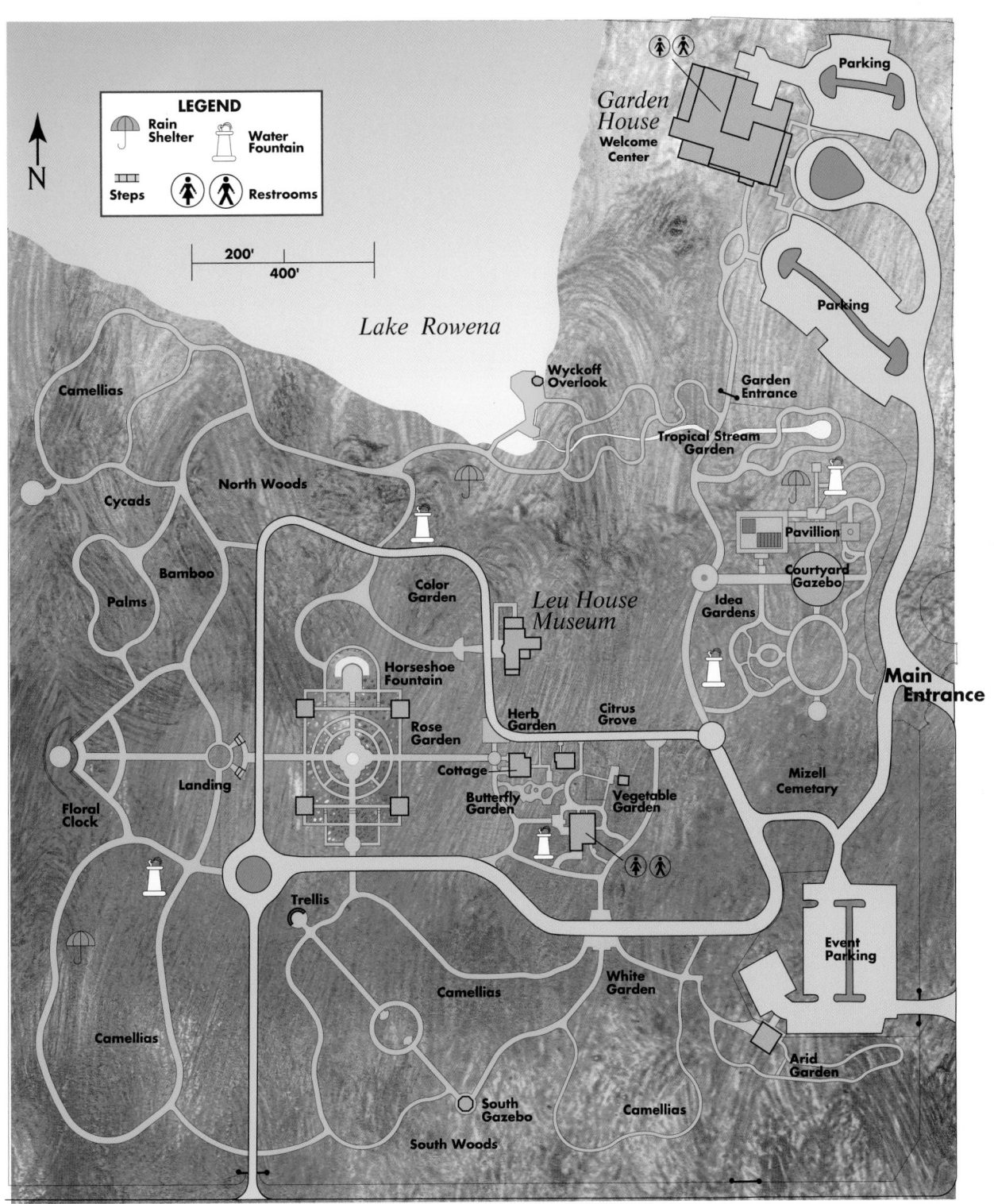

HARRY P. LEU GARDENS MAP

FOREWORD

GARDENS OFTEN REFLECT A PASSION FOR A SPECIAL PLACE and provide historical evidence that this special place has been cherished over many years. This is certainly the case with Harry P. Leu Gardens. With a fortunate orientation on the south side of Lake Rowena, the 50 acres that now comprise the garden offer an unusually warm microclimate with a beautiful lakeside view. The owners of the property—and eventually the builders of the magnificent historic home that stands there—were important figures in the history of Orlando. Harry P. Leu, however, was the visionary who left this special place for all of us to enjoy.

From 1936 to 1961, Harry P. Leu and his wife Mary Jane developed an extensive garden on the shore of Lake Rowena. This was a private and personal place of beauty. In their selection of plants and in the design of the garden, they reflected the horticulture of the period as well as their own passion for plants and beauty. Having selected a site protected from cold

weather in the winter and covered with the shade of grand old live oaks, their garden was a superb collection of colorful exotic plants—specifically roses, azaleas, and camellias—that rivaled any in Florida at the time.

The idea of dedicating a garden to the public was not a new idea, but certainly a generous one. We are fortunate that Mr. Leu was so forward thinking.

Above: Painting by Greta Baxter. Left: Photo by Kim Warden.

He recognized the value of public gardens to the cultural richness of a community and knew that the citizens of Orlando would benefit not just from a park in their city but, a beautiful garden. How grateful we are that he had this vision!

In 1961, residents of Orlando and visitors to our city were able to visit the Harry P. Leu Gardens and discover what gardening in Central Florida was all about. They could see the broad variety of plants that grow here. They could learn how to maintain them and get a sense of just how magnificent these plants would be when they reached maturity. With beautiful views of Lake Rowena and gorgeous trees, the garden was an important year-round destination.

There were seasonal surprises, too. In winter, Mr. Leu's extensive collection of camellias came into bloom and, with rich colors and exquisite form, decorated the garden from October to March; many of his original plantings exist in the garden today. Trumpet trees signaled early spring, brilliant colorful expanses of azaleas followed, and then the fragrance of citrus flowers announced that summer was on its way. Summer was filled with flowering gingers and bromeliads, orchids, and roses. Each season highlighted a different area of the garden with different plants blooming.

No garden remains the same. Trees grow. Hurricanes and freezes let us know that nature will prune and thin more aggressively than we ever would. However, a garden with a beautiful site, a foundation of native species, and an inspired vision can offer to the public a unique resource. Today, Harry P. Leu Gardens is more beautiful than ever.

Top and middle: Plant sale. Leu Gardens. Bottom: Storytime.

Top right: Summer camp. Right: Plant sale.

We are grateful to the strong collaboration that has been created by the staff of Leu Gardens with the Florida horticultural industry and public gardens across the United States as many new plants are acquired through generous gifts. Today, with more than forty different major collections of plants, the collection of camellias stands out as the largest documented camellia collection in eastern North America.

Botanic gardens throughout the world have important responsibilities to education and research as well as to presenting a well-documented collection of plants. Leu Gardens honors each of these responsibilities. By testing plants for the climate of Central Florida, we have better knowledge of what we should and should not plant. By offering a broad range of seminars for adults and programs for school children, Leu Gardens reaches out to the community with messages about the environmental, health, and economic benefits of plants and gardening.

As we reach our important anniversary year, let us not forget the very basic emotional connection we as human beings have with plants and gardens. It is at this important treasure of a garden in Orlando, Florida, that we are privileged to connect over and over again in each season of the year to the natural beauty of our unique part of the world. How fortunate we are! Congratulations, Harry P. Leu Gardens, on your 50th Anniversary!

**Above: Ghost stories.
Camellia show.**

**Top right:
Enabling garden.**

**Bottom right:
Movie night.**

KATY MOSS WARNER
President Emeritus, American Horticulture Society

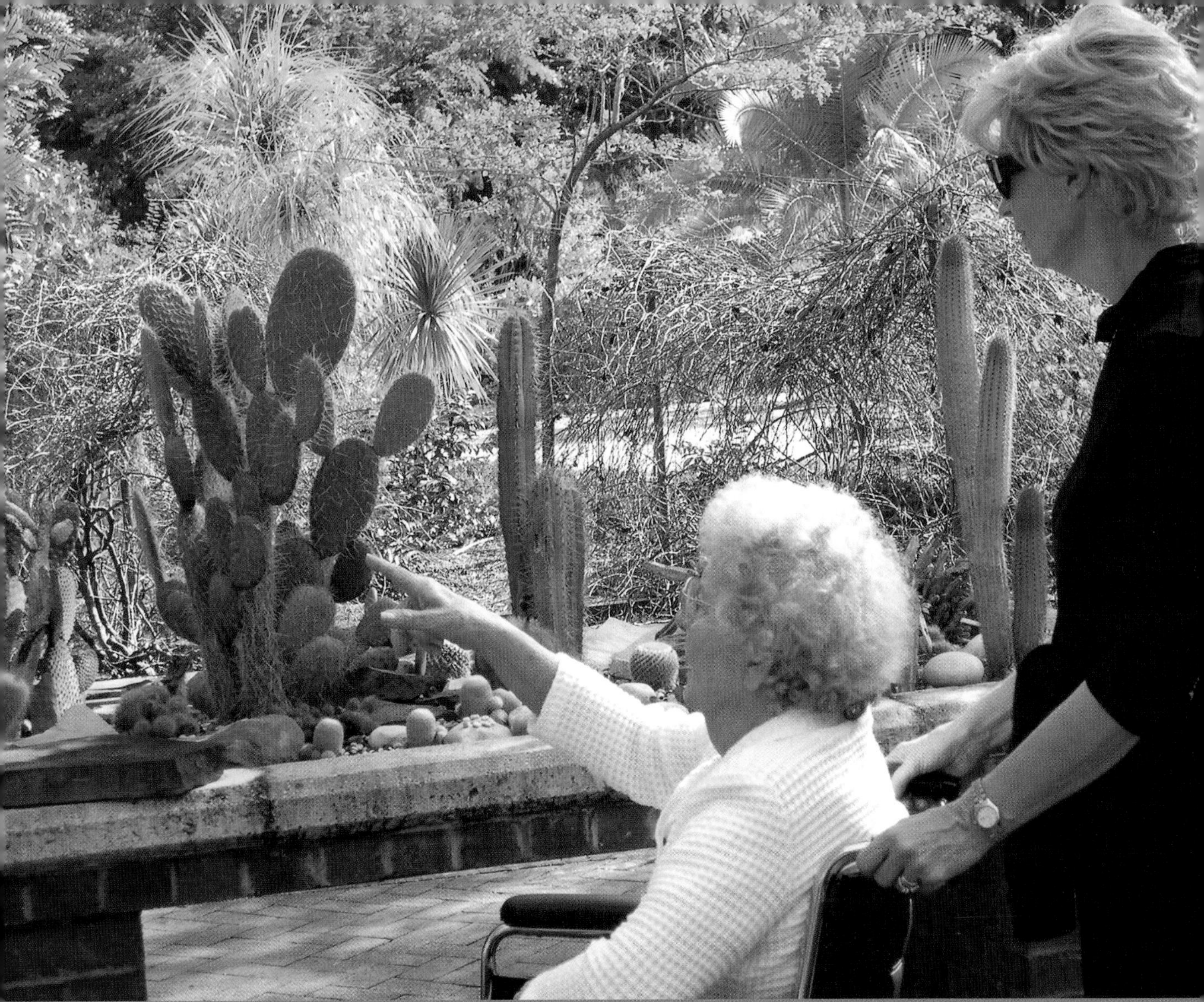

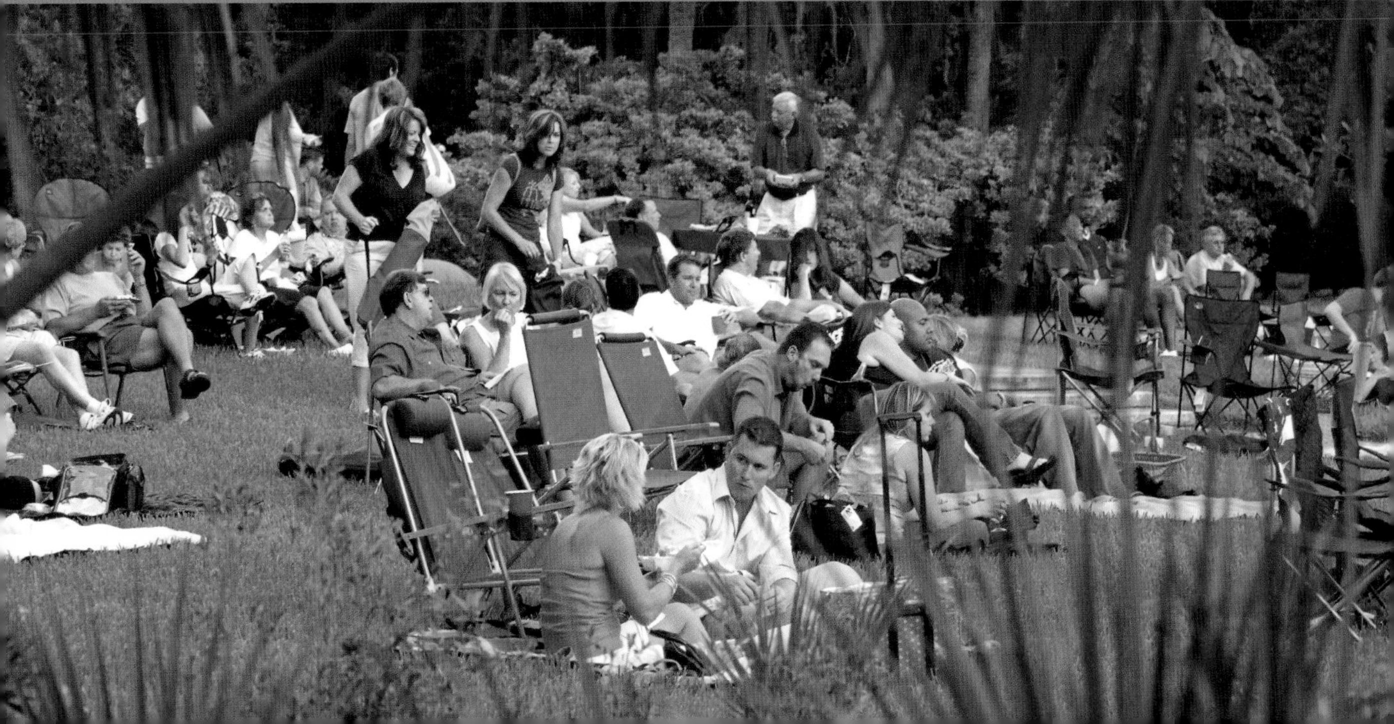

INTRODUCTION

WELCOME TO HARRY P. LEU GARDENS!

The City of Orlando and the Central Florida community has been blessed to have this beautiful and enduring treasure, and we hope this book inspires you to explore its stunning range of unusual specimens. Situated in a unique historic setting, Leu Gardens is more than a botanical collection: It's a living museum that presents new botanical finds, educates visitors about plants that thrive in Central Florida, and preserves important historic links to the past.

The children and adults who attend our daily educational programs have helped Leu Gardens play an important role in our shared community memory. We are proud of the fact that generations of Master Gardeners and backyard weekend warriors have found design inspiration and gained practical "how-to" knowledge from their visits to Leu Gardens.

We know Leu Gardens is much more than simply something to see. That belief is underscored each time couples gather for a moonlit stroll and an evening of jazz music; it's part of the inherent promise of every wedding and whenever families with excited kids roll out their blankets on the lawn to watch a movie on a clear summer night. Leu Gardens has borne quiet witness to countless special, spontaneous, and important moments in the lives of Central Floridians. That interaction—the shared memory of a perfect magnolia blossom or the sultry scent of an ancient rose combined with

Photo by Deborah Knispel.

12

watching a baby take those first steps on one of our garden paths—is what resonates in the lives of people.

Leu Gardens has a rich history dating back over one hundred years. Originally owned by the Mizell family, the property was purchased by Duncan Pell of New York who pieced the current acreage together and planted it with citrus. Harry P. Leu bought the property from the Joseph Woodward Trust in1936 and transformed it into a lush garden environment. The many exotic plants and numerous varieties of camellias for which the garden is famous are the result of the Leus' extensive world travel.

The heart of the Gardens is Harry and Mary Jane's home, known as the Leu House Museum, which has been meticulously restored and is on the National Register of Historic Places and open for tours. The Leus loved to open their property up to the public to enjoy the beauty of the gardens. In 1961, they deeded the house and their beautiful gardens to the City of Orlando as a lasting tribute to the city they loved and credited for their success. The deed came with the stipulation that the property must remain a nonprofit botanical garden, used solely for the enjoyment and education of the people of Central Florida.

KEITH OROPEZA
Chairman, Board of Trustees, Harry P. Leu Gardens

Photo by Ellen Zaslaw.

Each of us on the Board of Trustees, the staff, and the hundreds of volunteers who keep the Gardens beautiful encourage you to become part of this remarkable living museum. Stroll back in time, bring your family, and learn how to create your own garden or care for your favorite plant. Discover the solitude of a shady bench tucked away in a corner and embrace what Harry P. Leu understood: A beautiful garden can soothe your soul, nourish your creative spirit, and be a powerful common bond shared by generations.

Above: Storytime.
Right: Painting by Gene Amoroso.

HISTORY OF
HARRY P. LEU GARDENS

The property between downtown Orlando and Winter Park that is now
Harry P. Leu Gardens has a known history of more than one hundred fifty
years. David and Angeline Mizell were the first white settlers at a time when
much of Florida was inhabited by Seminole Indians. The Mizells built a small
cabin and established a farm on the property between 1858 and 1862.

The property was probably heavily wooded with pines and oaks, and they would have cleared part of the land for crops to feed their growing family; they may have also grown citrus on the property since orange groves were flourishing in the region.

In 1868, David was appointed the eighth sheriff of Orange County; however, he was killed in the line of duty a year and a half later, which left Angeline a 32-year-old widow with seven young children. In 1888, Angeline and David's son, John Thomas Mizell, constructed a modest two-story farmhouse that would eventually become the core of the Leu House. The farmhouse had a parlor and kitchen on the first floor and three bedrooms on the second floor; although it did not have plumbing or electricity, it provided a comfortable home for the Mizell family. Over the years, the Mizell family was important in the early development of Central Florida and family members would also include a judge, a county commissioner, and a state legislator.

The Mizell family farmed the property until 1902, when several parcels that now include Harry P. Leu Gardens were sold to Duncan C. Pell of New York. The sale may have been due to the lingering financial effects of the freeze of February 7, 1895, which destroyed citrus groves across Central Florida.

Left: Harry P. and Mary Jane Leu. Top: David Mizell. Above: Mizell homestead cabin.

Duncan Pell was a member of a socially prominent New York family and had settled in Orange County in late 1894 with his first wife Anna and their two children. They were part of a new group of migrants to Orlando—wealthy northerners seeking respite from cold winters. Orlando's cultural offerings included social clubs, polo, ballroom dances, and fine dining. Sometime in 1895, Anna returned to New York; Duncan filed for a divorce in Florida in 1901, and married Helen Gardner within a week of the divorce becoming final in 1902.

Above: Leu House Museum. Top right: Joseph Woodward.
Bottom right: Harry P. and Mary Jane Leu.

Duncan purchased the property to create a home for himself and his new wife, and immediately added two wings that doubled the size of the house. Electricity was also added, which made it a comfortable country home suitable for entertaining out-of-town guests. Citrus groves surrounded the house; horses, chickens, pigeons, pea fowls, and a mule were kept on the property. A polo field was constructed by Isaac Hopper south of present-day Corrine Drive and, following polo matches, Duncan most likely entertained friends on the property. In 1906, Duncan Pell sold his estate to Martha and Joseph Woodward of Birmingham, Alabama. Following the sale of the property, Duncan and Helen separated.

In 1909, the Woodwards acquired an additional parcel from R. Baylor and Stannye O. Hickman that included a 12-acre orange grove and a frame cottage. The Woodwards named their property La Belle, after the Woodward family's iron ore company. They also enlarged the house and constructed several outbuildings, including a three-car garage near the present-day Herb Garden for the new horseless carriages. Today, that building is known as the Garden Cottage.

The Woodwards maintained several citrus groves on the property. A visitor would have entered the property from Nebraska Street and driven down the sandy drive past the groves

Top: Mrs. Leu's bedroom.
Above left and right: Kitchen.

Right: Curator's office.

and numerous old oaks. After Joseph's death in 1917, Martha continued to use the country home as a winter residence, and after Martha's death in 1928, the property was rented and eventually sold to Harry P. Leu in 1936 as a home for himself and his wife, Mary Jane.

Harry P. Leu was born in Orlando and operated a local industrial supply business. He attended grammar school in Orlando, and then attended St. Joseph's Academy, graduating in 1901. He then traveled to New York and studied business, and in 1904, he returned to Orlando and began working for the Cain & O'Berry Boiler Company as a bookkeeper, timekeeper, shipping clerk, and "trouble shooter." He eventually became the sales manager, and by 1925, he was the major stockholder and changed the company's name to Harry P. Leu, Inc.

The Leus remodeled and redecorated the house, including modernizing the electrical wiring, plumbing, and kitchen. Today, the floor plan of the Leu House remains mostly as it was when Mary Jane and Harry lived there.

At the time that Harry purchased La Belle, the property was heavily wooded except for the citrus groves, and the Leus set out to transform the property into a garden estate; they focused on camellias, roses, gardenias, azaleas, and other flowering shrubs and trees. Avid travelers, they brought back plants and seeds from all over the world, including exotic species they hoped would thrive in the warm Florida climate. Harry's favorite plants were camellias, and by 1961, the gardens included 1,536 camellias and several hundred azaleas. The Leus also kept pens for fifty Asian pheasants, a dozen peacocks, turkeys, and guinea hens near what is today Forest Avenue.

In 1961, the Leus opened their gardens to the public by allowing cars to drive through. Later, the Leus negotiated with the City of Orlando to preserve their gardens as a public botanical garden. The Leus agreed to deed a majority of their property to the City for a token $58,018.73 even though the appraised value was in excess of $1,000,000. On December 21, 1961, the Leus deeded their gardens to the City as Harry P. Leu Gardens. In 1967, Orlando acquired an additional 8.8 acres from the Harry P. Leu Foundation to add to the Gardens.

The City engaged a landscape architect to prepare a master plan for the Gardens, and he planned a series of ten gardens. In 1965, the City pledged $100,000 annually for the next five years to develop the property. The City officially dedicated the Leu estate to the public on March 8, 1970, after investing nearly $700,000 into the development of the property. Initially, the tradition of allowing cars to drive through was continued; however, by 1971, the City prohibited cars and only allowed pedestrian access.

In 1971, the Floral Clock donated by the Kiwanis Club was installed, and in 1979 a four-tiered stone fountain from Italy was placed in the Rose Garden. In the 1980s, the Arid Garden was added, and in 1987 the Wyckoff Overlook was dedicated. The 1980s also brought the restoration of the Leu

TROY FINNEGAN
Board of Trustees, Harry P. Leu Gardens

House, creating Orlando's first historic house museum. In 1995, the Leu House and two other buildings on the property were listed in the National Register of Historic Places.

In 1995, the new Garden House was opened. The Garden House now serves as the welcome center for the Gardens and as a gathering place for horticulture groups, civic organizations, educational forums, banquets, and conferences.

Above: Sitting room.

Top left: Living room. Bottom left: Screened porch. Above: Dining room.

CENTRAL FLORIDA
GARDENING

To many, gardening in Florida conjures up images of vibrant tropical plants, exotic and colorful birds flying among palm trees, and lazily sipping rum-laced drinks in a shady hammock once the yard work is done. While that may be true in many of the areas of the state, in Central Florida, and Orlando specifically, the pace is much faster. Busy interstates, active neighborhoods, stimulating nightlife, and an energetic downtown create a tempo, a pulse if you will, that is full of life.

Even as far back as the early 1960s Mr. Leu could feel the quiet, calm manner of his Orlando changing. The tranquil rhythm of his native town was shifting. Clearly something had to be done to help remind everyone who lived and worked in Orlando of a gentler time—a time when pleasantries like casual strolls through gardens and learning local history were important.

Fortunately for those of us who live here and for those hundreds of thousands who now visit every year, Mr. Leu decided in 1961 to donate his home and beautiful garden to the City of Orlando.

Left: Photo by Deborah Knispel. Above: Spring plant sale.

By allowing everyone to walk along the paths of his 50-acre expanse dotted with magnificent live oaks draped in Spanish moss, Mr. Leu continues to give us hope that we, too, can create our own little paradise. He reminds us as we stroll through his garden that Orlando may in fact be the Shangri-la of gardening. Our soils are well drained, and we receive more than 60 inches of rain every year. Couple that with only occasional freezing temperatures, and it is a prescription for growing beautiful plants. Subtropical plants flourish in our ever-present bright sun, and warm temperatures help plants grow to astounding heights. Likewise, because of intermittent cool temperatures, we have the ability to grow many plants that are more commonly seen in temperate areas of the world. One could say we are on the "botanical cusp" of tropical and temperate plants.

Even though I have lived in Orlando for nearly eighteen years and in Florida for nearly thirty, I still cannot get accustomed to seeing bright green, luxurious banana plants laden with deep golden fruit growing alongside towering examples of camellias. Although I enjoy seeing tropical and temperate plants growing together (one can design stunning combinations), it just doesn't seem right. But that's the fun of growing plants in Orlando. Full sun gardens filled with plants adapted to the sometimes overwhelming heat overflow with bold colors of deep orange, crimson red, and majestic purple. Plants with exotic names like

Top: Photo by Pam Daum. Above: Photo by Jilene Williams. *A Walk Through the Park*.
Right: Photo by Joan Sandler. *Burst of Spring*.

Tibouchina, *Tabebouia*, and *Brilliantasia* make up the tropical palette. Shade gardens are more reminiscent of southern gardens, festooned with the rich plant palette of camellias, gardenias, and azaleas.

It is that contradiction that makes Leu Gardens a very special place. While a place for contemplation, it is also a location to attend one of more than thirty special events each year. Even though many visit for solitude, many others attend one of the nearly four hundred weddings or one of more than two hundred educational classes.

Make no mistake, however, it is the plants and the historic home that take center stage at Leu Gardens. For twenty-five years Mr. and Mrs. Leu lived quietly on their 50-acre estate. It has been said that it took Mr. Leu nearly five years to convince Mrs. Leu to live "way out in the country"—a location long since landlocked by urban development. Luckily for all of us Mr. Leu had the vision to create a regional treasure that will be a wonderful place to enjoy for generations to come.

ROBERT BOWDEN
Executive Director, Harry P. Leu Gardens

Left top: Photo by Grayson Olachew. *Shady Road*.

Above: Photo by Ellen Zaslaw.

CAMELLIAS IN LEU GARDENS

JERRY CONRAD

Camellias and Harry P. Leu fit together like a hand in a glove. His special love for camellias began when he started landscaping not long after he purchased the property in 1936. He went on a quest to obtain the best and biggest plants he could find and often brought mature specimens to Orlando by the train carload. He planted what he needed and sold the rest to friends and neighbors. The result is a dual benefit for Orlando because hundreds of plants were planted in the area as well as in his gardens.

Mr. Leu had a special love for pink camellias, and today we see his many 'Debutante' and 'Cameo Pink' varieties. His was not a large collection in terms of varieties; they were what he was able to obtain from nurseries in North Florida and South Georgia. However, he did find some rare varieties that are little known today, such as 'William Penn', a true purple and white that is popular when it can be obtained, and 'Madame de Strekaloff', a variety almost unknown today.

Mr. Leu's camellias were all planted under an existing forest of oaks and pines. After the Leus donated the Gardens to the City of Orlando, the collection languished for some years, but in the 1980s some local camellia lovers began to realize what a treasure it was. Under the guidance of Gary Paul there was a move to expand the collection with some of the new spectacular Reticulata Hybrid camellias, but most of them only

Left: *Camellia japonica* 'Donkelari'. Above: *Camellia japonica* 'Mary Jane Leu'.

survived a few years in our climate. Some of the best varieties of the 1950s and 1960s including 'Mrs. D. W. Davis', a variety developed in Seffner, Florida, and 'Faith', which came from Mississippi, were donated and still thrive.

In the 1990s Shaun Martin, Leu Gardens' first botanical record specialist, began to catalog all the plants in the Gardens. One Saturday I was invited to be with a group of area camellia growers to identify many of the unknown varieties. One concern was that the southern part of the garden, in particular, had become very dark due to the growth of the oak canopy, and the lack of light was beginning to hurt the growth of the camellias.

During this time, some of us noted that many of the camellias were not named varieties but seedlings that had sprouted beneath the vast collection of camellias. Most were only average semi-double flowers, but some had real merit. We wanted to find one to name for Mary Jane Leu, and in 1995 a miniature pink-and-white flower was registered with the American Camellia Society in her honor. (See page 35.)

Above: *Camellia japonica* 'Demi Tasse'. Right: *Camellia sasanqua* 'Pink Dauphin'.

Mother Nature decided the issue of an aging, overcrowded canopy in 2004 with Hurricanes Charlie, Francis, and Jean. Many of the aging trees were destroyed, and we felt panic as the camellias experienced minor leaf burn. Winter came along, however, when camellias are less likely to burn. Then spring arrived, and new growth came out everywhere. The camellias not only adapted to the increased amount of light but thrived! We were reminded that camellias are not forest plants but forest edge plants that like a few hours of sun each day. Today the collection is in the best condition since Harry P. Leu donated it, and it is improving yearly.

Much of the camellia world feels Central Florida is too far south for camellias. Local collectors know better, and the weekends when the camellias are in bloom attract some of the largest crowds of the year to the Gardens. Camellias are again showing up in our landscapes, thanks to Harry P. Leu's incredibly generous gift to the people of Central Florida.

Plans for the future are to add to the collection of older varieties, varieties that were introduced prior to 1940. In addition, some of the newer varieties thrive in our Central Florida climate and are being added. The collection now is one of the finest in the United States, with camellias found throughout the Gardens. The future has never been brighter for camellias in Central Florida.

Top: *Camellia japonica* 'Mathothiana'. Above: *Camellia japonica* 'Scented Sun'.

Left:
Camellia sasanqua
'Setsugekka'.

Below:
Camellia sinensis.

Next page:
Camellia japonica
'Pink Perfection'.

Right:
Photo by Tiffany Martin.

Below:
Camellia 'Freedom Bell'.

Camellia japonica 'Anita'.

CAMELLIAS

THE COLOR GARDEN

ROBERT BOWDEN

The Color Garden is where a wide variety of brightly colored annuals and the occasional perennial plant can be seen blooming every month of the year. The emerald green backdrop of broad-leaved evergreen shrubs and trees in the Color Garden creates the setting for wedding pictures taken in the adjacent Rose Garden.

Flowering plants of every description are festooned with flowers of every shape and size in the Color Garden (sometimes called the Annual Garden or Display Garden). To determine their suitability in our climate, the plants located in this garden have been grown elsewhere throughout the Gardens for several years in smaller numbers. (A popular spot to test new varieties of annual bedding plants is the Idea Garden near the Tropical Stream Garden. Here the flowers can be placed in shade, semi-shade, and full sun locations and in a wide variety of soil types ranging from clay to quick-draining sand.) In addition, many new perennials from growers and hybridizers throughout the world are sent to Leu Gardens and are tested in the Idea Garden and as elements in mixed containers located throughout the property. Once they have proven to be hardy in Central Florida's weather, they are then grown in much larger numbers and placed in the Color Garden for display.

Left: Photo by Suzanne Darby. *Essence of Color.*

Above: Photo by Richard Koch. *Garden Path.*

The garden area immediately adjacent to the horseshoe fountain
is generally planted with soft, pastel colors of cantaloupe, light pink,

apricot, light blue, and white. Leu Gardens is host to more
than four hundred weddings annually, many of which occur
within the northern horseshoe terminus of the Rose Garden;
the colors of the annuals planted in the wedding site are
more neutral than those found elsewhere throughout the
garden so they don't clash with a wedding's color scheme.
Because the northern end of the Color Garden functions as
the backdrop for the wedding, the colors there are bright and
powerful so they can be seen in photographs from across a
large expanse of lawn. Flowers there are usually taller and run
the palette of deep orange, red, purple, blue, and white. The
flowers often include varieties of Mexican marigolds, sunflowers, princess
flowers, hibiscus, lantana, and cleome.

The western edge of the Color Garden sits in deep shade most of
the afternoon, but because it is not included in wedding pictures, the
horticulture staff can be a bit more creative in their combinations of color
and textures. The growing conditions there are not nearly as harsh as
they are at the north edge, and more interesting varieties of plants can be
seen. An unusual but perfectly suited ginkgo tree, one of earth's very first
seed-producing plants, is located between the path and the annual flowers
on the west edge of the garden.

Above: Photo by Marlene Rimensberger. Right: Photo by Suzanne Darby.
Aging Beauty.

Photo by Grayson Olachew. *Hidden Wings.*

Photo by Grayson Olachew. *Playful Garden*.

Fabric illustration by Ellen Linder. *Natural Progressions.*

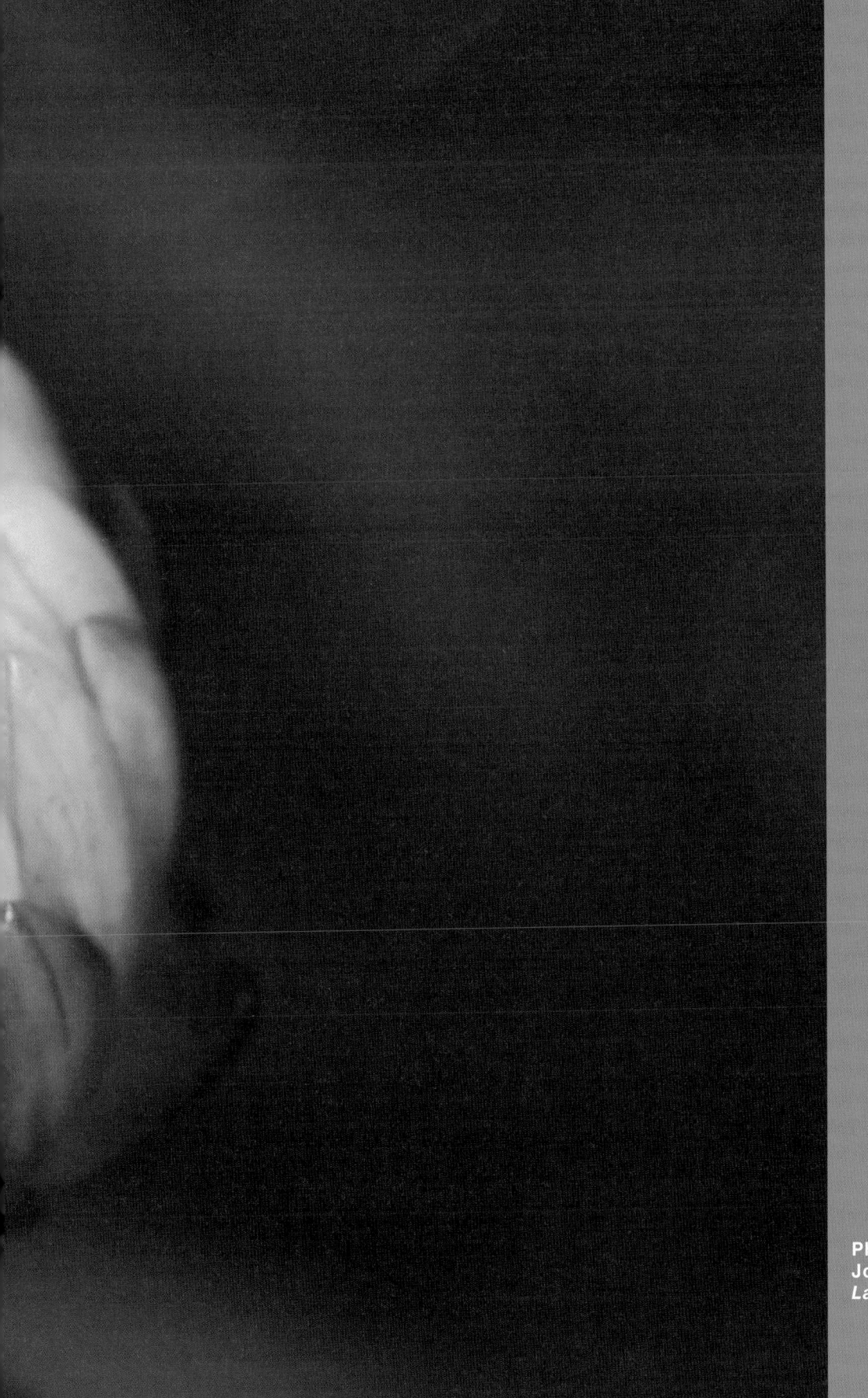

Photo by
Joan Sandler.
Late Bloomer.

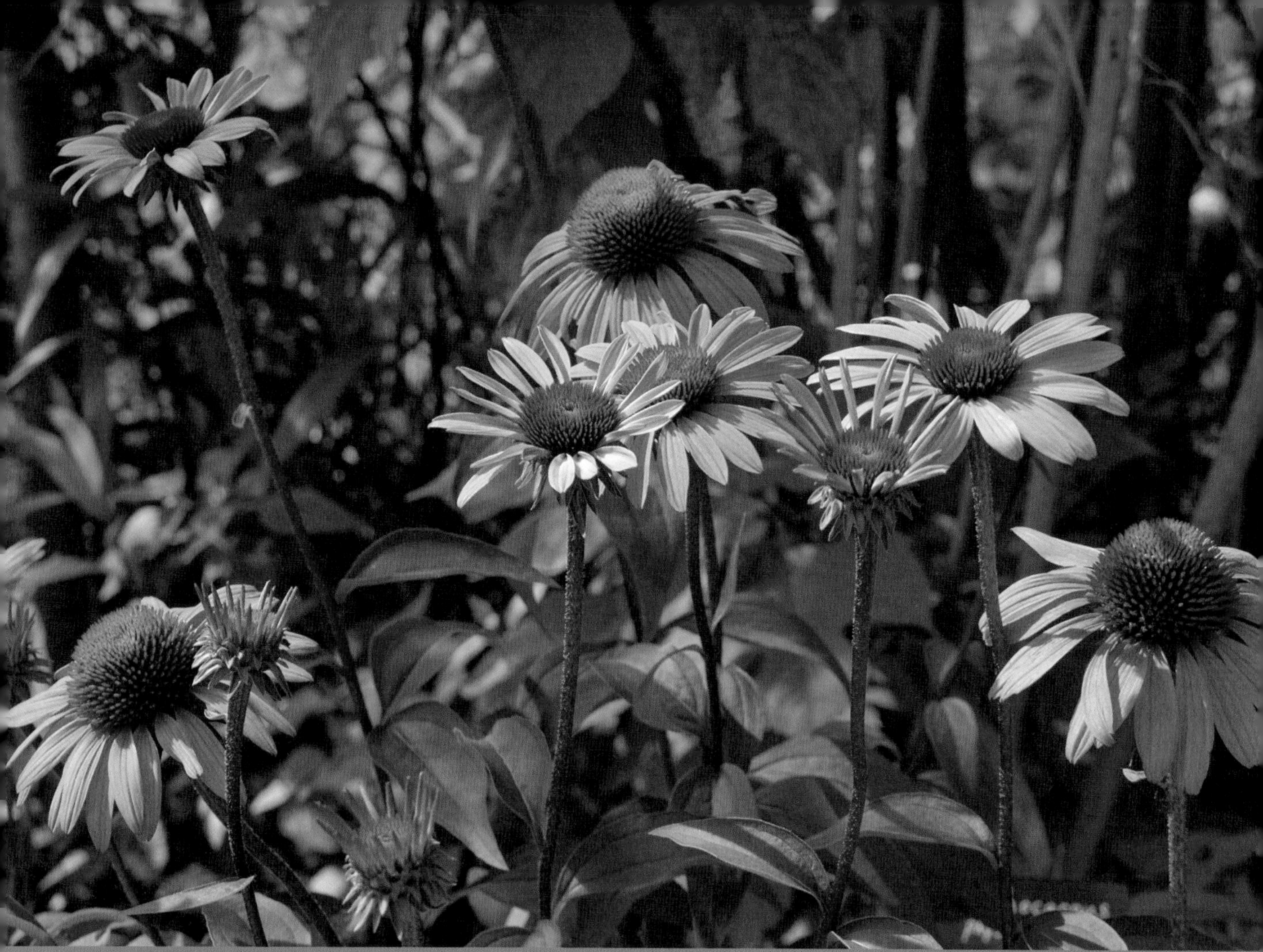
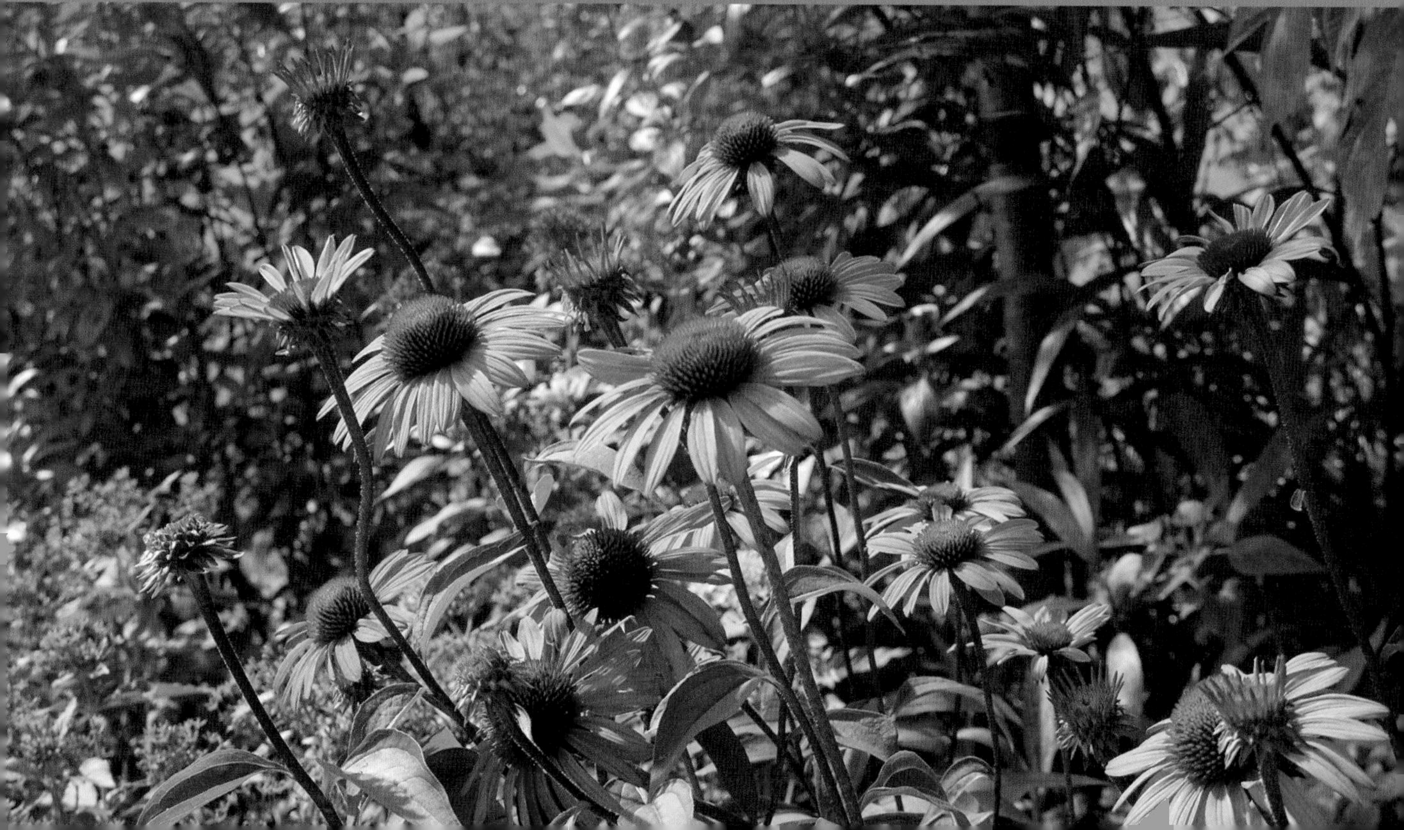

The tunnel-like entrance at the eastern edge of the Color Garden is created by two opposing 30-foot-tall lavender crape myrtles underplanted with dwarf mondo grass with spots of color provided by seasonal mixed containers. Similar to those plants on the western edge, the bedding plants in the eastern area prefer some shade during the day—the eastern border plants get shade in the morning and full sun in the afternoon. The backdrop of evergreen plants along the eastern border include a dwarf variety of camellia named 'Shishigashura' and a semi-dwarf (to 6 feet tall) variety of firebush (*Hamelia patens* var. *glabra*).

All photos by Kim Warden.

Above: Photo by Kim Warden.

COLORS

THE ARID GARDEN

MARY DeFISHER

The beautiful Arid Garden of today was originally just a dusty, barren pathway from the old visitor's center to the conservatory. In the 1980s, the conservatory (a small fiberglass house where tender tropicals, including orchids, were displayed when they bloomed) was one of the main draws to the Gardens. To improve the entry, staff drew up plans to establish a desert garden. Thus was born what was then called the Xerophytes Garden and is now called the Arid Garden.

Left: Bull's horn acacia. (*Acacia spaercephala*.) Below: Aerial view.

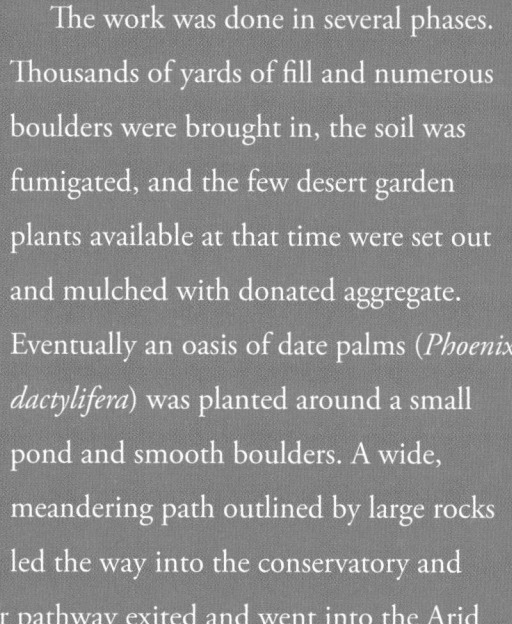

The work was done in several phases. Thousands of yards of fill and numerous boulders were brought in, the soil was fumigated, and the few desert garden plants available at that time were set out and mulched with donated aggregate. Eventually an oasis of date palms (*Phoenix dactylifera*) was planted around a small pond and smooth boulders. A wide, meandering path outlined by large rocks led the way into the conservatory and another pathway exited and went into the Arid Garden proper.

As the public becomes more water conscious, appreciation of water-conserving plants increases. Exposure to new arid plantings through tours and classes develops public interest, gives visitors new ideas for landscaping, and increases demand from nurseries and mail order houses.

Above top: Cochineal cactus. (*Opuntia cochenillifera*.) Above: Sotol. (*Dasylirion texanum*.) Right: Blue candle cactus. (*Myrtillocactus geometrizans*.)

We've grown many beautiful flowering trees that have adapted to our climate: *Ceiba speciosa*, *Cordia boiseri*, *Erythrina grista-galli*, to name a few. *Agave americana* (also called the century plant) in its many forms has delighted us with its 30- to 40-foot stalks of flowers. Then there are many low growing succulent plants: sedums, *Euphorbia* (most commonly the crown of thorns and its many hybrids), and the stinky *Stapelia*. Of course,

some of these arid plants have also succumbed to Florida's afternoon rains and the occasional winter freeze. Cacti, for example, can usually survive some frosts as long as the soil is kept perfectly dry, but Mother Nature seems to water the earth just before she sends frigid cold.

The garden was officially dedicated in 1986, but it continues to be a work in progress. Each year new plants and trees are introduced, thanks to the plant-hunting staff. Failures are recorded and replaced, and new flora is set out for the evaluation and enjoyment of Leu Gardens' visitors and patrons.

Top: Baja fairy duster. (*Calliandra californica*.) Above: Photo by Dave Wood. *Sedum*.

Top: Tequila agave. (*Agave tequilana*.) Above: *Aloe vera*.
Right: Variegated prickly pear. (*Opuntia cochenillifera* 'Variegata'.)

Above: Photo by Dave Wood. *Yellow Barrel Cactus.* **Below: Dyckia. Right: Photo by Dave Wood.**
Crown of Thorns.

ARID

THE BUTTERFLY GARDEN

JOEL ARANT

One surefire way to get young people interested in gardening is to set aside an area for butterflies. In 1998, the horticulture staff did just that in a location near the cottage. Several dozen different plants, carefully selected for their ability to provide food for caterpillars and nectar for butterflies, were planted one summer. Before the end of the day, five different types of butterflies had discovered the tiny haven planted for them. The small garden was an instant success—not only for the butterflies but also for the guests now able to view them!

In 2002 the area set aside for butterflies was included in a major redevelopment of what the horticulture staff calls the "inner core" of the garden. The Butterfly Garden, an integral part of the Gardens' education programming, was enlarged, and it is now host to more than one hundred different kinds of plants. Rough-hewn flagstones mined from a century old quarry in North Georgia were placed with Orlando's very own street brick, creating pathways that meander through the garden. For the first time, larval shrubs and trees were planted among the host of bedding plants and herbaceous perennials to complete the kind of visual display so desirable in an educational exhibit.

Left: Photo by Lea Patenaude. Zebra longwing. Above: Photo by Suzanne Darby. *Colorful Discovery.*

In 2006, in response to requests, Leu House Museum docent Heywood Brown created a beautiful box to display the various butterfly chrysalises. Mr. Brown has been known for many years as the Garden's resident clock expert, and his beautiful chrysalis box is reminiscent of an old Swiss chalet, paying homage perhaps to Mr. Leu's ancestry. The children loved the chrysalis box so much that another was installed in 2009. Chrysalises are removed from various places in the garden to protect them from predators and displayed in the boxes until the adult butterflies emerge and are released.

Below: Photo by Marlene Rimensberger.

Left: Photo by
Lea Patenaude

Far left: Photo by
Kim Warden.

The Butterfly Garden is festooned with flowers and shrubs of every description and many are host-specific; that is, specific plants will attract a specific butterfly. The large orange barred sulfur butterfly, for instance, had never been seen at Leu Gardens until a subtropical shrub called *Senna bicapsularis* was planted. Two days later the brightly colored butterfly appeared.

The southern edge of the Butterfly Garden is planted with a camellia relative, *Ternstroemia gymnanthera*, that was purchased from Glen St. Mary's Nursery—the same nursery from which Mr. Leu purchased many of his plants in the late 1930s.

Pentas, an old Florida favorite, in red, pink, lavender, and white, attract a large number of nectar-seeking butterflies including monarch, queen, cassia, sulfur, peacock, and swallowtail. A variety of vines including *Passiflora*, or passion flower, attract a number of leaf-eating caterpillars including the bright orange gulf fritillary and zebra longwing. Pipevine swallowtail caterpillars gorge themselves on many varieties of pipevine (*Aristolochia*) and often completely strip the plant of leaves (the vine sprouts new leaves a few days later). A few smaller trees were planted in the garden, including many varieties of senna (*Cassia*), and paw paw (*Asimina*) to attract the zebra swallowtail.

Photos by Lea Patenaude.

The garden is a living laboratory. The large purple hairstreak feeds upside down on flowers of the bog sage (*Salvia uliginosa*) to escape predators. This butterfly has long wispy "tails" on its hind wings and waves them back and forth as it feeds. The antennae-looking tails have a large dark spot that often fools predators (lizards, small birds, and so forth) into thinking the insect's head is in a normal location—on top. When it strikes, the predator gets a mouthful of wing and the butterfly is able to escape.

Skipper butterfly.

Likewise the queen butterfly has evolved a wing pattern and color similar to a monarch to evade predators in a process called "mimicry." The larvae (caterpillars) of the monarch butterfly eat the leaves of the poisonous milkweed plant (*Asclepias*) and as a result taste bad. Despite the queen butterfly's appetite for anything but milkweed leaves, it resembles a monarch so most predators leave it alone.

Because insecticides of any kind would be harmful to butterflies at any stage of their life cycle, they are not used in the Butterfly Garden. As a result the space has become a haven for a wide variety of insects and small animals. In addition to butterflies and moths, ladybugs, colorful bees, and praying mantises share the garden with lizards and tree frogs … and children of all ages!

Above: Photo by
Lea Patenaude.

Left: Photo by
Julia Sigmore.

Upper left: Photo by Lea Patenaude.

Far left: Tree frog.

Left: Photo by Julia Sigmore. *Bee on leaf*.

Above: Photo by Marlene Rimensberger. *Green anole lizard*.

Photos by Lea Patenaude.

BUTTERFLIES

THE HERB GARDEN

CHARLES CLARK

Let's stroll the pathways of a special place at Leu Gardens … the Herb Garden. Picture that it's early morning, and we step through the arch that leads to the Herb Garden.

First we come upon a garden sage with dew glistening on its leaves. Nearby a rhythmic peeping sound tells us a cardinal is searching for a morning meal. As we look down the pathways we see some sprightly mint; nearby a comfrey spreads its ample green leaves around a brace of pretty little white flowers. Fennel is in full bloom behind it. As we look from side to side, clumps of horsetail, Mexican tarragon, nasturtiums, epazote, basil, pineapple sage, and chamomile can be seen. We see garlic and French chives, and some salvias interspersed in the beds proudly showing off their red, blue, and pink flowery heads.

As the day slowly warms, monarch, fritillary, longwing, and swallowtail butterflies flutter back and forth. A beautiful monarch rests on the white umbel of a yarrow plant while another sits on an orange-and-yellow-flowering milkweed. Maybe a chrysalis will appear and a life cycle will begin again.

Some of these herbs are interwoven with many wondrous plants on display in the other gardens. For example, the Butterfly Garden boasts many herbs, while our Herb Garden has plants loved by butterflies. The adjacent Vegetable Garden has chiles, fruits, savory, and many other herbs growing in its beds. On our walk on other Leu Gardens pathways we can stop to note gingers and juniper.

Left: Photo by Charles Clark.

To fully experience what the herbs have to offer, we need to use all our senses. Rub the leaves, brush by the plants, enjoy the delicate texture of the flowers. For me, rubbing the underside of a ginger leaf can relieve tension and put me in a better state of mind than any medication. Rubbing some of the other herb leaves releases their oils and brings forth glorious aromas beyond those we detect wafting from the flowering herbs.

While walking the pathways, it's fun to identify the flowers and foliage plants that excite our taste buds. Another fun challenge can be to see how many herbs we see that are used for healing, such as purple coneflowers (*Echinacea*), foxglove (*Digitalis*), valerian (*Valeriana officinalis*), aloe vera (*Aloe vera*), and many more.

Mornings are not the only good time to walk the Herb Garden pathway; each time of day can bring different pleasures. Cooler afternoon or twilight visits can be very relaxing. Also, each season brings an entirely different set of experiences to the senses, because different herbs thrive in different seasons to bring a new collection of sights, smells, textures, and tastes.

To fully appreciate the Herb Garden at Leu Gardens I like to walk the pathways many times because I am always amazed at what I missed before. Each trip brings to light another treasure, plus there can be other

Above: Society garlic flower. (*Tulbaghia violacea*.)
Right: Photo by Lea Patenaude.

positive observations. Perhaps you will have the fun of seeing moms and dads, grandmas and granddads, or a group of wide-eyed fourth graders.

A good friend and herbalist once defined an herb as "any useful plant." Herbs can be used in cooking, medicinally, industrially, for their aromas, and more. I feel that strolling repeatedly along the Herb, Butterfly, and Vegetable Gardens, as with all the pathways at Leu Gardens, is akin to revisiting a masterpiece painting. Each viewing brings me new insights and new joys, as I expect it will for you.

Yet my favorite is the very special Herb Garden, a place, I feel, that has so many glories to impart to all ages, throughout different seasons, and during diverse times of the day. I sincerely hope you will take the time to walk through that arch and share a very special experience.

Above and Right: Sweet basil 'Lettuce Leaf'. (*Ocimum basilicum*.)

Swallowtail caterpillar on fennel.

Sweet basil. (*Ocimum basilicum.*)

Photo by Charles Clark.

Above: Herb garden.

Right: Curled-leaf and Italian parsley. (*Petroselinum*.)

Left top: *Echinacea* 'Ruby Giant'.
Left bottom: *Salvia blepharophylla*.
Above: Arizona milkweed. (*Asclepias angustifolia*.)

Above: Eastern swallowtail on *Tithonia*.

Above: Herb garden.

HERBS

THE VEGETABLE GARDEN

CECIL HAWLEY AND JOEL ARANT

T he Vegetable Garden at Harry P. Leu Gardens is designed to represent the gardens created by families that lived on the property and to showcase the produce they grew, harvested, and ate. In addition, the garden educates visitors by growing more modern vegetables that can survive and thrive in Central Florida.

The Mizells, who lived on the property in the 1800s and were the first known settlers, practiced subsistence vegetable gardening since there was nothing in the area at the time to supply the ingredients necessary for a well-rounded diet. Subsistence gardens are, by and large, grown with varieties that are preserved for future use, and even though food is harvested and eaten daily, the main function of these plantings is to provide out-of-season vegetables by preserving them through canning or curing. Some of the vegetables in this category include black-eyed peas, snap beans, corn, squash, sweet potatoes, Irish potatoes, and greens.

Vegetable gardens in Central Florida in the 1800s were not adjuncts—they were necessities! Also necessary was the involvement of extended family and neighbors to supply the extra labor to ensure timely harvests, which was reciprocated throughout the community until all crops were harvested and preserved. The food gardens of those times did not have a wide range of vegetable varieties; only crops that could survive the harsh environment of Central Florida were used. Large harvests were necessary to feed large, hard-working families, and all heavy work was powered by horses or mules. During harvests even school was suspended so all could assist.

Above: Photo by Suzanne Darby. *Past and Present*.

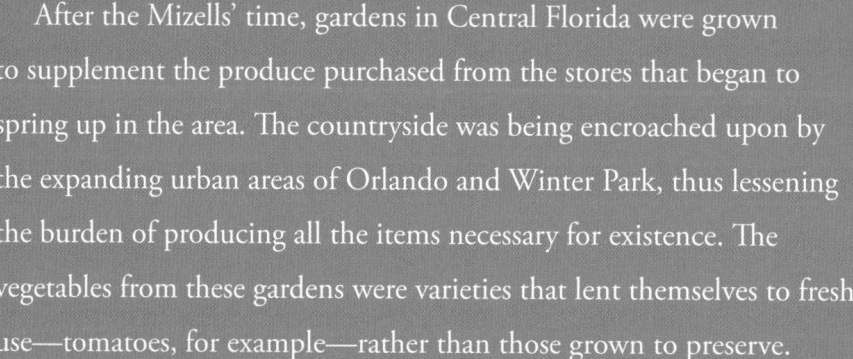

After the Mizells' time, gardens in Central Florida were grown to supplement the produce purchased from the stores that began to spring up in the area. The countryside was being encroached upon by the expanding urban areas of Orlando and Winter Park, thus lessening the burden of producing all the items necessary for existence. The vegetables from these gardens were varieties that lent themselves to fresh use—tomatoes, for example—rather than those grown to preserve.

The mother and children usually tended these gardens, while the father worked off the property providing income to cover living costs. Most of the vegetables from these gardens would be eaten fresh, since canned goods of out-of-season vegetables were readily available. Gardening became more enjoyable, not just a necessary chore, although gardening in Florida is never easy, even with modern methods. Insects, diseases, weather, and other problems plague the vegetable gardener and will continue to do so. The trained gardeners who tend our small demonstration garden today continue to deal with challenges and disappointments.

With the establishment of the Vegetable Garden, showcasing heirloom varieties of vegetables used in the 1800s and early 1900s was paramount, so the Vegetable Garden at Harry P. Leu Gardens is a mix of heirloom (or at least open-pollinated) varieties and modern hybrids. Open-pollinated varieties were used in turn-of-the-century gardens to ensure a stock of seeds for the following year's crops. Hybrids, on the other hand, need to be replaced each year from an off-site source, since

Above: Photos by Gino Ferreira. Right: Photo by Deborah Knispel. Citrus garden.

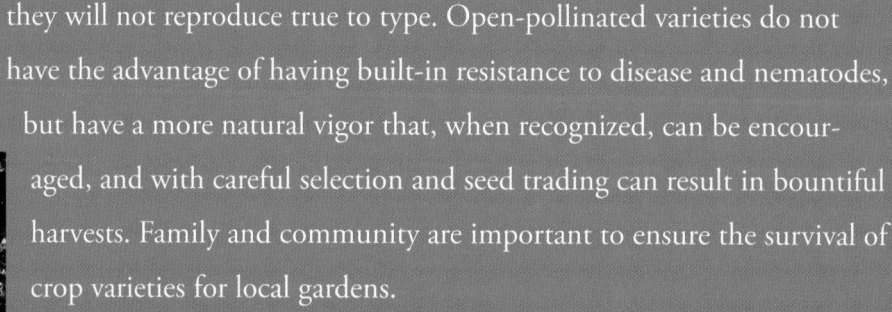

they will not reproduce true to type. Open-pollinated varieties do not have the advantage of having built-in resistance to disease and nematodes, but have a more natural vigor that, when recognized, can be encouraged, and with careful selection and seed trading can result in bountiful harvests. Family and community are important to ensure the survival of crop varieties for local gardens.

Displaying heirloom varieties grown by early pioneers of Florida and the families who lived on the property allows visitors to the garden to see what they can still grow in their home gardens. Many of these heirloom varieties originated from other countries—watermelon, okra, and sorghum from Africa, for example. Asia provided us with lettuces, sweet peas, onions, radishes, and cucumbers. From the Americas came bush beans, flint corn, eggplant, potatoes, tomatoes, and peppers.

In Central Florida, the best time to grow a garden is during the cooler months. Starting in August, planting cool-weather crops such as cabbages, lettuce, and kale helps ensure a good harvest. Carrots, peas, radishes, squash, spinach, and tomatoes also can be grown at this time.

The Vegetable Garden at Harry P. Leu Gardens, while small, still manages to provide a wide variety of vegetables to a local food kitchen for distribution. Each year we provide approximately one thousand to fifteen hundred pounds of vegetables (including citrus from our demonstration grove) for this purpose.

Top: 'Sunhome' nectarine. Above left: 'Burpee Bibb' lettuce. Above right: 'Big Red' mustard. Right: 'Medusa' ornamental pepper.

Above: 'Tah Tsai' mustard. Right: 'Veronica' broccoli.

Above: 'Silver Queen' corn.
Right: 'Bonnie Hybrid' cabbage.

VEGETABLES

THE ROSE GARDEN

MARTY PAWLIKOWSKI

Some plant species attract horticulturalists, botanists, and collectors due to their rarity. Roses, on the other hand, appeal to a wide variety of people—their beauty, blooming propensity, and the fond memories they often evoke are among the many reasons. A rose stirs us to sniff its bloom; its inspiring beauty and alluring fragrance draw us in. Without the rose— perhaps the most identifiable flower in the world and the national flower of the United States—the collection at Leu Gardens would be incomplete.

The collection, known as Mary Jane's Rose Garden after Mary Jane Leu, was placed in several locations near the Leu home before its current location was built in 1944. In 1990, the Rose Garden was renovated and expanded, and the garden plantings increased to more than three-quarters of an acre, nearly doubling the garden's original size.

The garden design is in the classic formal European style with a fountain centered upon the intersection of two axes—a major north/south axis intersected by a minor east/west axis. The rose collection is planted in beds radiating out symmetrically from the central fountain in concentric quartered rings. From the south entry you are led down the long axis past the central fountain to a lower plaza terminating in a crescent pool; multiple geysers are framed by a colorful mass planting of floribunda roses and a display garden in the background. It is absolutely breathtaking when the garden is in peak bloom.

Left: Photo by Karen Constantine. *A Garden Beauty*. Above: Illustration by Amy Green. *Rose Garden Gazebo*.

Mary Jane's Rose Garden is reported to be the largest formal rose garden in Florida. But its size, as defined by aerial extent or quantity of roses in the collection, is not what makes it important; what places it on the must-see list is its educational benefit for Florida rose-growers.

The collection includes a partial representation of the following classes of roses: Hybrid Tea and Grandiflora (typically one large bloom on a long stem like a florist's rose); Floribunda and Polyantha (typically multiple blooms produced in sprays on each stem); Shrub (a class of rose that combines the bloom shape and character of old garden roses with the vibrant colors of modern roses); Old Garden Rose (roses introduced before 1867, the year the first Hybrid Tea rose was introduced); Miniature (typically very small rose blooms and plants); and Climbing Rose (a class not identified by bloom type but by growth characteristic).

Above: Photo by Elaine Pawlikowski. Right: Photo by Marlene Rimensberger.

In each of these classes of rose varieties, the Leu collection presents a sampling that can be successfully grown in Florida's climate. These varieties are continuously evaluated for their hardiness, ability to bear many flowers, and disease and insect resistance. A variety in the collection today may be gone in a year or two if it performs poorly in one or more of the evaluation criteria.

Rose cultivation can be classified as a love of labor. Of course, how much labor depends on where you fall in the rose world … gardener, connoisseur, or somewhere in between. In Florida's landscape, no other plant species can match a rose's prolific year-round flowering.

Properly tended roses perform substantially better than neglected roses. However, roses in the collection are not "pampered" because Leu Gardens incorporates integrated pest management practices and utilizes the cultural strategies of the typical home gardener. As a result, the varieties grown in the garden are roses that should perform well in any garden in Florida.

Also noteworthy is that the rose collection is grafted on *Rosa × fortuneana* rootstock. In the late 1950s, Dr. Sam McFadden performed rootstock research at the University of Florida that found that roses grafted onto × *fortuneana* rootstock grow larger, produce a more vigorous plant and more flowers, are more resistant to Florida's nematodes, and live much longer than on other rootstocks.

Left top: Photo by Robert Ravas. *Paint the Roses Red*. Left bottom: Photo by Darlene Torres.

Above: Photo by Lisa O'Brien. Right: Photo by Elaine Pawlikowski.

Our experience at Leu Gardens supports the use of × *fortuneana* as a rootstock. From the planting in 1990 to the mid-1990s, the health and vigor of roses that were not grafted to × *fortuneana* declined, and portions of the collection were lost as a result of the inferior rootstocks.

Of special interest in the garden are the "Bermuda Mystery Roses" found within the collection of Old Garden Roses. These roses were discovered in Bermuda, and the original name or source of the rose is unknown, thus the use of the name "mystery." These Bermuda Mystery Roses may be sports (genetic mutations) or hybrid seedlings (a cross between roses) of Old Garden Roses. Bermuda Mystery Roses are named, in most cases, after the owner of the garden or the location where they were found and have flourished for at least a century. This collection is significant as it represents roses that have survived years of neglect growing in a tropical and semitropical region, that are highly resistant to both nematode damage and fungal diseases, and that are floriferous in Florida's hot humid weather.

Over the past fifty years Mary Jane's Rose Garden has welcomed countless visitors who come for many reasons: To share the beauty of the roses with a loved one; to seek solitude and escape from the stress of everyday life; to discover a special variety they hope to include in their own garden. Whatever your reason, visit often. Come and experience a most beautiful flower, the rose.

Top: Photo by Elaine Pawlikowski. 'Baronne Prevost'. Above: Photo by Elaine Pawlikowski. 'Belfield', a Bermuda Mystery Rose.
Right top: Photo by Julia Sigmore. Right bottom: Photo by Kim Warden.

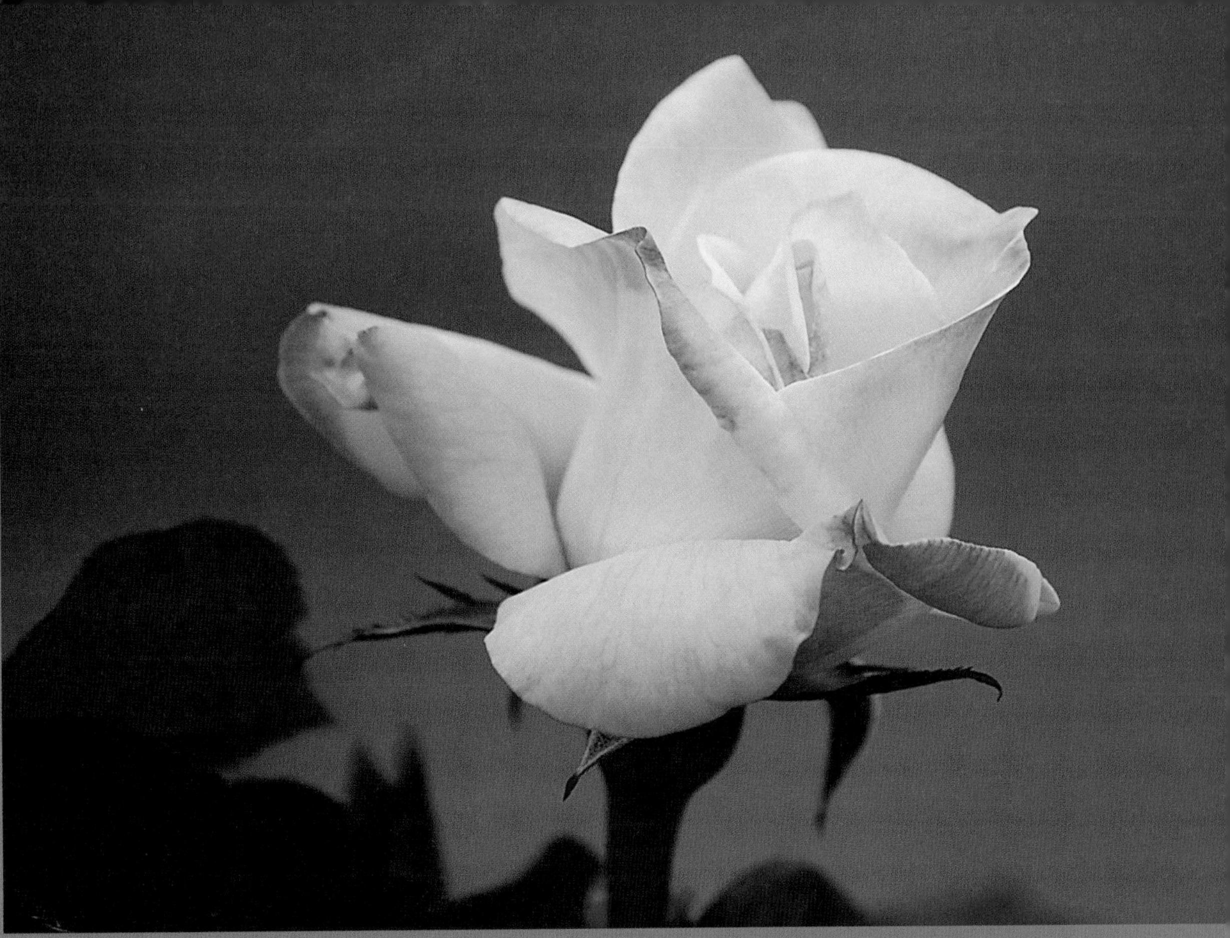

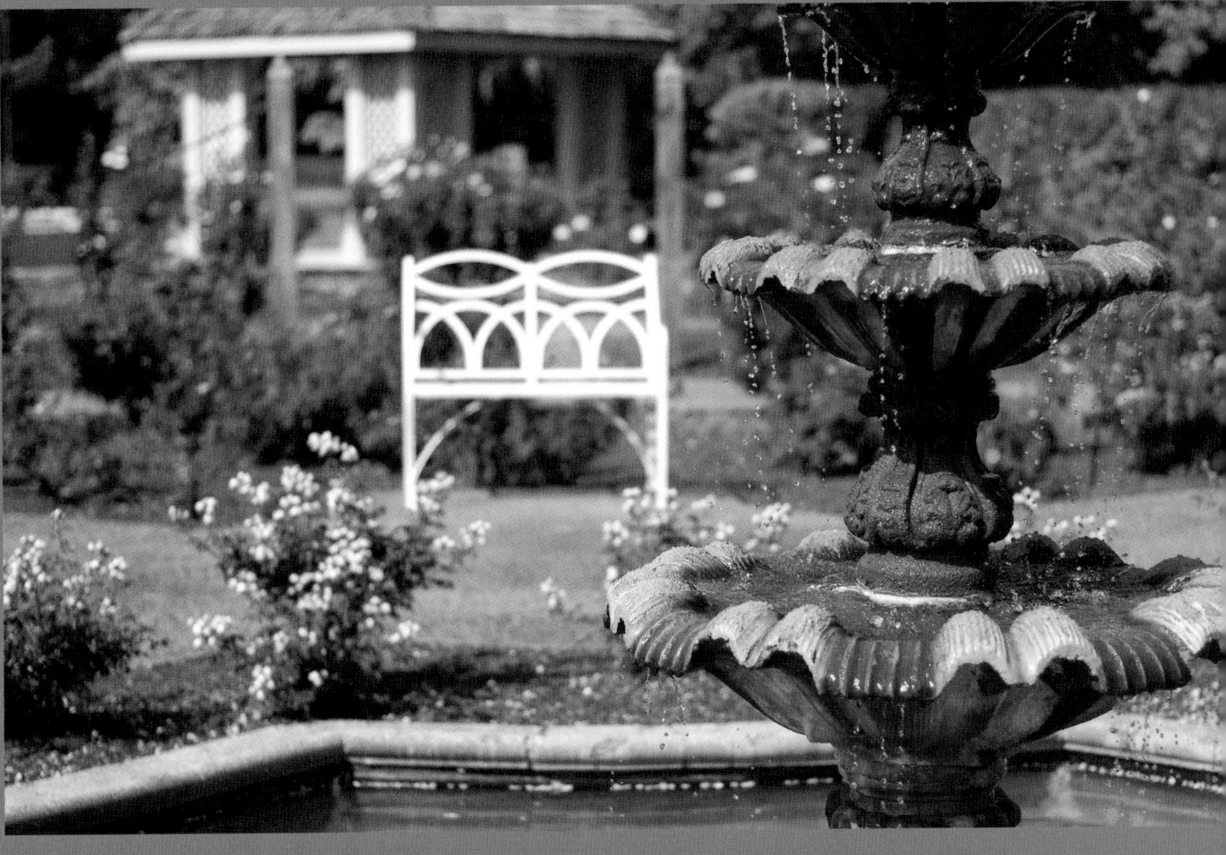

Photo by Elaine Pawlikowski. 'Tropical Sunset'.

Photo by Marlene Rimensberger.

Photo by Kim Warden.

Above: Photo by Suzanne Darby. *Purity*. Right: 'Dainty Bess'.

ROSES

THE IDEA GARDEN

GREG MEYER

Designed for gardeners of all types and physical abilities, the Idea Garden is a true outdoor classroom for "how-to" gardening in Central Florida; the 3-acre site was designated a unique outdoor classroom in 2000. Whether you're a novice or an experienced green thumb, there is always more to learn. Visitors to the Idea Garden find that learning is fun and easy!

The learning experience in this outdoor classroom includes not only gardening the way we may traditionally think of it—as planting and caring for plants—but also includes other aspects of the garden environment that make this a unique and educational experience. This includes demonstrating how to effectively use hardscape materials in the garden, an open air exhibition building used as a gardening classroom, raised planters for hands-on gardening instruction, and many examples of garden furniture and art displayed throughout.

There are many examples of hardscape materials (pavers, bricks, concrete, gravel, and stone) that can be used in a garden setting and these are vividly demonstrated in the main entry courtyard; here, visitors can see and understand how the hardscape of a garden can add color, texture, and a sense of place to their garden environment.

Left: Painting by Cindy Sturla. *Leu Gardens Courtyard*. Above: Photo by Deborah Knispel. *Leu Amaryllis*.

Another unique part of the Idea Garden is the open air exhibition building used for cooking demonstrations, often using fresh herbs and vegetables gathered directly from the garden. This open-air building is also used by school groups on field trips as a classroom, and is a place to escape the sometimes too frequent inclement weather experienced in Central Florida. The structure was designed architecturally in a "Florida vernacular" style and blends in well with the overall scale of the Idea Garden. It serves as the "main house" of the garden and provides a backdrop for the entry courtyard and for the outdoor idea patio garden.

Perhaps one of the unique features of the Idea Garden is the raised planting beds that provide hands-on interactive involvement for all. The planting beds provide a true learning experience where gardeners get their hands dirty as the Leu Gardens staff leads classes. The therapeutic effects of gardening are well known, and this part of the Idea Garden opens up the value of gardening to all, which is why the raised beds were designed to be fully accessible and are ADA compliant.

Above: Photo by Julia Sigmore. *Father and Kid Statue*. Right: Photo by Deborah Knispel. *Leu Couple*.

Peter Olsinski
American, 1950–
Bride and Groom
2002
Mixed Media
Purchased by
Friends of Harry P. Leu Gardens

Garden furniture and artwork are key components of any garden setting and these are showcased throughout the Idea Garden. Visitors are given the opportunity to experience various examples of garden benches, chairs, fences, gates, pottery, trellises, and other garden furniture, and can then plan how to implement these ideas into their own garden setting. Artwork is also prominently displayed to show how art can inspire and enhance the home garden experience.

The Idea Garden at Leu Gardens is truly a unique and valuable resource to the gardening community of Central Florida. Whether you are a veteran gardener or just getting started, you can learn how to appreciate the value a garden can bring to your home. Besides the informative hardscape garden courtyard, the outdoor class-rooms, site furniture, and art examples show-cased in the Idea Garden, there are also many other garden examples to learn from—the bird garden, water garden, patio garden, wild flower garden, perennial garden, native plant garden, and shade garden, to name a few. In these "idea" gardens visitors can see and experience varied garden expressions that may relate to their own home environment.

Photos by Deborah Knispel.

Photo by
Deborah Knispel.

131

All gardens should inspire a connection with the earth and to the environment and remind us of our need to be good stewards of the planet. Gardening is also an expression of care and an art form. The Idea Garden at Leu Gardens expresses these ideas in a very real, informative, and hands-on way. The success of this particular garden experience is not so much in the garden itself, as wonderful and beautiful as it is, but is more about how to inspire the visitor to garden at home and enjoy the beauty gardening can bring to each of us.

Above: Photo by Gino Ferreira. Right: Photo by Tiffany Martin. *Dainty*.

Above: Photo by Kim Warden. Right top: Photo by Richard Koch. *Golden Tree*.
Right bottom: Photo by Jilene Williams. *All Is Well*.

Above: Photo by Joan Sandler. *Graceful Awakening*.
Right: Photo by Suzanne Darby. *Focused Fern*.

IDEAS

THE NATIVE WETLANDS GARDEN

KELLEY PETERMAN AND JULIA NORAN

Nestled in a residential setting on the shores of Lake Rowena, Harry P. Leu Gardens has a diverse collection of exhibits, but the Native Wetlands Garden is a favorite area for many guests for a number of reasons.

While strolling along the winding path and absorbed by the lush "tropical" jungle, the first-time visitor might believe this walk was carved out of a native forest, but the simple truth is every plant, streambed, rock, and sidewalk was carefully planned and laid out. Native plants were chosen to fit what would have historically occurred in this area on the slopes of Lake Rowena.

The benefits of native plants are numerous and well documented. They require less water and less maintenance, and they help prevent the introduction and potential propagation of exotic seeds. The establishment of a native plant garden at Leu Gardens educates visitors by showcasing a number of commercially available native plants that can easily be purchased and incorporated into a home landscape.

In the beginning, this area was riddled with exotic plants, and the first step was to have all plants hand removed and to selectively treat the nuisance exotic vegetation. Some of these species, such as camphor trees, had been intentionally installed, but other nuisance plants, such as wild taro and skunkvine, found their way into the garden on their own. Leu staff relocated the selected species and then treated the garden with water-safe herbicides prior to native plant installation.

Native wetland species such as pickerel-weed, giant bulrush, and maidencane were introduced into the wetlands area along Lake Rowena. In higher, drier areas, native vegetation such as coontie, wild coffee, and saw palmetto were installed through a combination of hand shoveling and soil augering.

Top: Saw palmetto. (*Serenoa repens*.)
Above: Yaupon holly. (*Ilex vomitoria*.)
Right: Pickerelweed. (*Pontederia cordata*.)

This garden has special meaning to us. Beyond designing it, we were able to get our hands dirty again working on it. Whether placing rocks in the waterfall or working behind the business end of a shovel, we feel our contribution—along with the hours of work by countless volunteers and professionals—made this garden a special place. We hope you will take time to enjoy the Native Wetlands Garden and to remember that some of the best gardens are simply natural.

Top: Giant leather fern.
(*Acrostichum danaeifolium*.)

Above: Photo by Julia Sigmore. *Water Lily*.

Right: Photo by Mason Katzen.
The End of the Line.

Far right: Tall ironweed. (*Vernonia gigantea*.)

Photo by Karen Kershaw.

NATIVE WETLANDS

THE PALM GARDEN

ERIC SCHMIDT

The Palm Garden contains more than three hundred species that belong to the Arecaceae or palm family. This fascinating garden also contains important collections of cycad and bamboo.

Originally, Mr. Leu planted this section as a tropical garden, with a major focus on palms but including other tropical plants such as a large roxburgh fig (*Ficus auriculata*), sausage tree (*Kigelia africana*), and toog tree (*Bischofia javanica*). After the property opened as a public botanic garden, the area became known as the Palm Garden, and more specimens were added to enhance the collection.

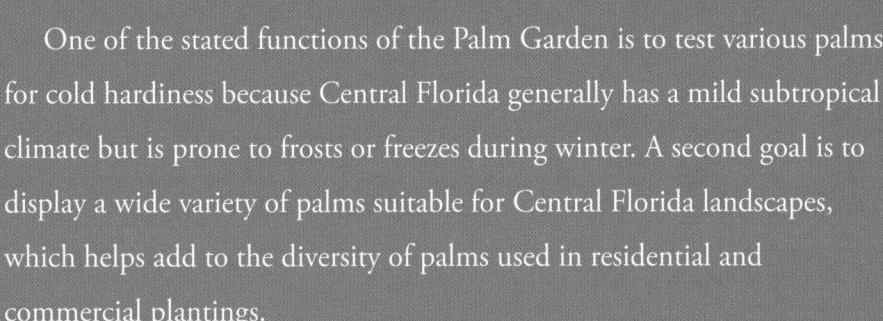

About 1995 it was decided to organize and plant the Palm Garden in a more educational manner. The palm family is divided into several main "tribes," so a plan was drawn up to plant members of certain tribes adjacent to each other so that palms with related features would be together and their features could be studied.

One of the stated functions of the Palm Garden is to test various palms for cold hardiness because Central Florida generally has a mild subtropical climate but is prone to frosts or freezes during winter. A second goal is to display a wide variety of palms suitable for Central Florida landscapes, which helps add to the diversity of palms used in residential and commercial plantings.

Left: Australian fan palm. (*Licuala ramsayi*.)
Above: Photo by Mason Katzen. *Lost in a Bamboo Forest*.

And the final goal is to demonstrate many of the economically important palms used by humans—as food, oils, waxes, fibers, thatching, and rattan. In fact, some palms are important to the survival of certain cultures, while others are viable economic crops in different parts of the world.

There are now a wide variety of palms to be found in the collection at Leu Gardens. Many are very ornamental or have interesting features or uses to them. The coconut palm (*Cocos nucifera*) is probably the world's most recognizable palm and a valuable landscape specimen. Found throughout the tropics and one of the world's leading economic crops, its fruit is used for food and oils, the leaves for fiber and thatching, and the trunk for building.

The date palm (*Phoenix dactylifera*) is native to the desert oases of northern Africa and Arabia. The fruit, which are known as dates, have been a staple food for thousands of years. The African oil palm (*Elaeis guineensis*) is native to the equatorial regions of western Africa. The fruit contains a seed with high oil content and is the source of palm oil, which is high quality and widely used in cooking and for industrial uses. Vast plantations of this palm are grown in tropical regions of Africa and southeastern Asia.

Above: Paurotis palm. (*Acoelorraphe wrightii*.)
Right: Photo by Pam Daum.

Above: Photo by Paul Wean. *Bamboo Shoots*. Right: Photo by Karen Kershaw. *Striped Bamboo*.

The leaves of the carnauba wax palm (*Copernicia prunifera*) yield the valuable carnauba wax. Native to wide areas of Brazil, its wax has a high melting point, is very durable, and is widely used in car waxes, candy coatings, and other industrial uses. The rattan palms belong to a large genus called *Calamus*. There are hundreds of species and a majority of these grow in huge thickets as clambering vines. Many grow thick stems that are flexible but durable, which are the rattan used for the making of furniture.

Besides a collection of palms, the Palm Garden at Leu Gardens contains the cycad collection and the bamboo collection. Cycads are an ancient group of plants that have existed for over two hundred million years and were one of the dominant plant forms when dinosaurs ruled the earth. Cycads are often called palms or confused with them, but they are not related to palms; cycads are gymnosperms (cone bearing) and are more closely related to ferns, ginkgos, and conifers. They are the most primitive of the seed bearing plants. Cycads belong to the Order Cycadales and comprise three Families: Cycadaceae, Stangeriaceae, and Zamiaceae. Many cycad species are threatened with extinction in the wild because of habitat destruction and from overcollection of wild specimens. One cycad is native to Florida, the coontie cycad (*Zamia floridana*). Other primitive plants can be found

Top: Photo by Mason Katzen. *A Long Way Up*. Right, clockwise: *Copernicia* bed; Natal cycad (*Encephalartos natalensis*); Chestnut cycad (*Dioon edule*); Photo by Robert Ravas. *Beyond the Garden Gate*.

amongst the cycad collection to help create a prehistoric atmosphere, including ferns, tree ferns, horsetail, *Araucaria*, *Ginkgo*, *Metasequoia*, and *Wollemia*.

Bamboo is a woody-stemmed plant that is a member of the grass family, *Poaceae*. Bamboo is found in a variety of climates and locations and is native to all continents except Europe and Antarctica, and it can range in height from a couple of inches tall to more than one hundred feet with canes greater than a foot in diameter. Bamboo is an extremely useful and important plant in its native lands with thousands of uses. There are two basic types of bamboo: clumping and running. Clumping bamboo is the more desirable type because it stays in dense clumps with the new shoots emerging within several inches. Running bamboo, on the other hand, can become a nuisance because the new shoots can emerge many feet away from the others. Almost all of the bamboo in the collection here at Leu Gardens is of the clumping type.

In the Palm Garden, the many clumps of bamboo provide screening or nice backdrops. They also function as windbreaks and have helped create a warm microclimate and provide protection on cold nights for the more tender palms growing in this area.

Top: *Arenga engleri* flower. Above: Lady palm. (*Rhapis excelsa*.) Right: Carnauba wax palm. (*Copernicia prunifera*.)

Above: Cardboard cycad. (*Zamia furfuracea.*)

Bismarck palm. (*Bismarckia nobilis.*)

PALMS

THE TROPICAL STREAM GARDEN

JAY HOOD

A lush, green garden today, the Tropical Stream Garden area was originally an overgrown ditch with broken, steep sidewalk sections and steps in disrepair. Identified in the Leu Gardens' Master Plan as an important component of the Gardens' entry sequence, it was neither safe nor inspiring for visitors to the Gardens at that time.

Early on, however, it was recognized there was a great opportunity to transform this degraded area into a feature garden. The steep slopes as well as significant existing plant specimens could be preserved in place and incorporated into a Tropical Stream Garden. This garden would serve as a dramatic entry statement to the rest of the collection and leave a lasting impression on the visitor. Part of the design process included the newly hired Executive Director, Robert Bowden. His love and passion for tropical plants made the "Ravine" garden complete, and overseeing the vast collection of tropical and subtropical plants was one of his first priorities for construction. A team of landscape architects was engaged to prepare construction documents for the design, and they worked seamlessly with Mr. Bowden and the garden horticulturalists to maintain the vision laid out in the Master Plan.

One of the challenges of the project was to create a fully accessible pathway to negotiate the slopes along the stream. The solution was to add a significant amount of "meander" to the walks and, where these large sweeping

Left: Photo by Lisa O'Brien. *Hibiscus*. Above: Photo by Richard Koch. *Solo Brush*.

turns occurred, the design team developed spring pools of still water to contrast with the moving stream water.

Today, this garden has dense plantings of lush herbaceous plants and shrubs. The path leads to a footbridge over the ravine, and from the bridge visitors have dramatic views up and down the lushly planted Tropical Stream Garden. Plantings include bird-of-paradise, banana, philodendron, ginger, tree ferns, palms, heliconias, and flowering vines with a tropical character. Recirculated water cascades from one pool to another. The bold forms, textures, and colors of the plants interplay with the stream as it courses its way down the ravine toward Lake Rowena. On the edge of Lake Rowena, the stream transforms into a display of native aquatic vegetation; here the visitor has the opportunity to pause and enjoy the expansive vista across the lake.

Guests are able to leave the primary path to wander along smaller walks that wind through the Tropical Stream Garden and along the stream. The garden also features small-scale bridges that allow for views over the top of the stream. Eventually the visitor arrives back at the main footbridge and, just beyond the bridge, visitors encounter a spectacular view across the forested lawn toward the Leu House. The primary path then leads away from the House; but visitors have been given not only an intimate tropical experience, but also a glimpse of things to come as they continue their journey through Leu Gardens.

Left bottom: Photo by Pam Daum. *Welcome to the Jungle.*

**Above: Photo by Ron Caimano.
Bat plant (*Tacca chantrieri*).**

Right: Photo by Ken Wallace.

Above: Photo by Ron Caimano.
Iris in Bloom.

Left: Photo by Kim Warden.

Above: Photo by Karen Kershaw. *Awakened.*
Right: Painting by Greta Baxter. *Light Around the Corner.*

166

Above: Fabric collage by Ellen Linder. *Ti Plants Aglow*.
Left: Photo by Lea Patenaude.
Right: Photo by Mary Balanda. *Powderpuff*.

TROPICALS

MEET THE AUTHORS

KATY MOSS WARNER is President Emeritus of the American Horticultural Society (AHS), a national, nonprofit, member-based organization with a bold vision of "making America a nation of gardeners, a land of gardens." Katy provided day-to-day leadership as President and CEO of AHS from 2002 to 2006 and served on the AHS Board of Directors from 1992 to 1998, serving as Chair of the Board from 1998 to 2000. Prior to that, Katy was the Director of Disney's Horticulture and Environmental Initiatives at the Walt Disney World Resort in Florida, responsible for the landscapes of four theme parks, fifteen resort properties, and over 70 miles of roads on the 30,500-acre property. From 1976 to 2000, her leadership helped sustain Disney's horticultural traditions of beautiful gardens and themed landscapes. She encouraged her team of over seven hundred specialists to share, with millions of visitors each year, the importance of beauty, the value of gardens, the richness of garden cultures, the necessity of growing food, and the challenges that face those who love the earth. Katy currently serves on the Board of "America in Bloom," a national awards program that encourages beautification in communities across America. Katy received a degree in landscape architecture from the University of Arizona in 1974.

KEITH OROPEZA is a fourth generation Floridian, with family roots in Key West. After graduating from high school in Miami, he went to college in Brevard, North Carolina, and finished at Louisiana State University, receiving a degree in Landscape Architecture. His design influence can be seen at almost every area theme park as well as local resorts. Keith's talents have reached far beyond the Florida coastline to include projects in Brazil, Costa Rica, Guatemala, Columbia, the United Arab Emirates, and China. He resides with his wife Kathleen and two young sons, Nicholas and Alexander, in Orlando, which he has called home for over twenty-seven years.

TROY FINNEGAN is a member of the Harry P. Leu Gardens Board of Trustees. He and his wife, Kathrine, own a home across from the Gardens on Nebraska Street and regularly visit the Gardens.

ROBERT BOWDEN has been the Executive Director of the City of Orlando's beautiful Harry P. Leu Gardens for seventeen years and earlier served as the Director of the Atlanta (Georgia) Botanical Garden and as the Director of Horticulture of the Missouri Botanical Garden in St. Louis, Missouri. Robert's delightful photographs and enjoyable essays can be seen in a wide variety of gardening magazines and professional journals. He appears often on several nationally syndicated television programs and is the author of several books including the *Guide to Florida Fruit and Vegetable Gardening* and the *Florida Gardener's Resource*, both published by Cool Springs Press.

JOEL ARANT is a former horticulturist at Harry P. Leu Gardens and maintained the Butterfly Garden, Herb Garden, and Vegetable Garden. Joel attended the University of Tennessee at Martin where he studied zoology and other sciences and received his B.S. degree.

CHARLES T. CLARK was the President of the Herb Society of Central Florida. Both he and his wife Lois are avid herbalists who have hosted a demonstration Home Garden in Orlando for nearly two decades. He has been a Central Florida businessman since 1971.

MARY DeFISHER was a frequent visitor to Leu Gardens for many years; when she attended the official dedication of the "Xerophytes Garden" (now the Arid Garden) in 1985, she decided to become a volunteer and has been with the Gardens ever since. Her real expertise and passion is in working in the Gardens' greenhouses and nurseries where she and other volunteers work every week, sowing seeds of new and unusual plants, transplanting seedlings, and ultimately creating inventories for the gardeners to plant in the Gardens. Mary also performs other volunteer duties, including mailing the Gardens' monthly newsletter, the *Garden View*. She has been recognized several times as the Leu Gardens volunteer with the most number of hours worked in a given year. The staff is very fortunate that Mary considers them her second family!

JAY R. HOOD, ASLA, has over twenty-two years of experience in site design and landscape architecture for public spaces. Jay has a B.S. in Landscape Architecture from Purdue University. His design influence is featured in the public realm design of places such as Lakeland's Hollis Garden, the City of Orlando's Harry P. Leu Gardens, Winter Park's Park Avenue, Downtown Plant Street in Winter Garden, and the University of Central Florida's Health Sciences Campus at Lake Nona. Jay focuses on functional and timeless design that is grounded in context and equity of users. Jay has long believed in the creative use of native plants and indigenous hardscape materials. His goal with every design is to create spaces that have meaning, tell a story, and create lasting value.

GREG MEYER, RLA, Principal of MSI Design Orlando, has over two decades of experience in hospitality and resort design, planning, and entertainment design. His attention to clients' needs helps cultivate creative design solutions that are unique, environmentally responsive, and integrated with each project's goals and budgets. Greg enjoys the interaction with his clients and the design team as the design process unfolds from concept to built reality. In addition to work throughout the United States and the Caribbean, Greg's portfolio includes projects in China and the Middle East. He received his Bachelor of Landscape Architecture in 1980 from the University of Florida.

JULIA NORAN is an Ecologist with four years of experience in the biological sciences. Julia holds a B.S. in Biology from the University of Louisville and a M.S. in Biology from the University of Central Florida; her thesis research focused on the composition of bird assemblages in Central Florida cypress domes. Julia's experience includes work in vegetative and hydrologic monitoring, wetland delineation, GPS data collection, GIS mapping and analyses, and threatened and endangered (T&E) species surveys.

MARTY PAWLIKOWSKI, a registered Landscape Architect, has been growing roses in Central Florida for the past twenty-five years with his wife, Elaine; both are American Rose Society Master Consulting Rosarians and Accredited Horticulture Judges. Marty served on the Leu Gardens Board of Trustees and is a past President of the Central Florida Rose Society, where he and Elaine have been members since 1989. Elaine is editor of *Wind Chimes*, the Society's newsletter, which has received several national awards. They have grown over three-hundred fifty different varieties of roses and introduced into commerce the roses 'Natasha Monet', 'Miss Ada', and 'Josi'.

KELLEY PETERMAN, PWS, is an Ecologist with expertise that includes ecological assessments of Florida flora and fauna, with a specific focus on wetlands and wildlife as they relate to both private land development and public policy. She is familiar with Lake Wales Ridge endemics and is in the process of negotiating a Habitat Conservation Plan (HCP) with the United States Fish and Wildlife Service (USFWS) for listed flora and fauna in this region. Kelley has helped create master plans for nature-based recreation for the Lake Harney Wilderness Area in Seminole County, DeBary Nature Park in Volusia County, and the Circle B Bar Reserve in Polk County. She is currently working with Osceola County to develop a policy for Habitat Management Plan requirements. Kelley has also managed all aspects of long-term monitoring of wetlands creation and enhancement, wildlife management, and protected species management plans.

ERIC SCHMIDT is the Botanic Records Specialist at Leu Gardens. He maintains the accession database for the plant collection, keeps plants labeled, helps oversee many of the collections, and obtains new plants to be added to the collection at Leu Gardens. Eric has an Associate's Degree in Environmental Horticulture from Valencia Community College in Orlando, Florida. He has lived in Orlando for over thirty years and has been a part of the Leu Gardens staff for over seventeen years.